OVERCOMING TRAUMA THROUGH AWARENESS AND EMPOWERMENT

Peter Kamau
OVERCOMING TRAUMA THROUGH AWARENESS AND EMPOWERMENT

Published by BooxAi
ISBN:978-965-578-505-0

OVERCOMING TRAUMA THROUGH AWARENESS AND EMPOWERMENT

PETER KAMAU

CONTENTS

Trauma disconnects the victim from life in the present moment. Cage the victims within and connects with the painful events of the past. This hand book helps to detect the hidden trauma. Exposes the invisible damage of trauma to society!

Educate on trauma. Call to trauma victims support framework in small and main sectors.

This book is the product of combined effort of committed helpers who used their experience to support and ensure the final manuscript is published effectively.

1. To my wife Jacinta Gachigi (RN,USA) for her Nursing knowledge contribution.

2. My children, Kennedy Gachigi (Statistician,USA), Timothy Gachigi (Computer scientist,USA.) and my daughter Treaser kiptoo (Nursing students,Florida,USA)

3.Dr Kanyi Gitau (Ophthalmologist) Muranga county Kenya, for his input.

4. Jennefer Kilel –Assistant professor -Liberty University,USA, for her contribution in knowledge.

5. Professor Antony Gachanja phD FRSC ,DSC (hon) (Lecturer) Jomo Kenyatta University,Kenya.

6. Titus Tarus, Director of Nursing-Moi University Teaching and Referral hospital -Kenya.

7.Denver Shelton (Rev)-Durham, NC ,USA-First Assemblies of God for his input.

8.Dr Mungai Munyaka (PHD), Lecturer - Mount Kenya University.

9.Ashley Hardee-RN, Central Regional psychiatric hospital Butner, NC, USA.

INTRODUCTION

Trauma informed care concept was highlighted in 1970, when doctors identified unusual phenomena. The Vietnamese injured war veterans were treated and physically healed.However, Symptoms persisted and thorough history taking and review ,doctors identified that although the war was over, it was not really over ,because their minds lived in the war zone. The war zones inflicted real emotional pain equivalent to the real situation. We all equally need knowledge and self-awareness to identify similar situations and overcome them through the knowledge from this book. It was not until 2013 when the WHO released an outline on trauma care guidelines and management. Overwhelming results have been achieved where trauma informed care has been applied.

However, the progress in implementation has been slow while traumatic events like war, earthquakes hurricane , floods and gun violence have escalated. Everytime a disaster occurs,Immediate disaster response is activated. Rescue workers ran to the site and offer food and shelter. The full arm of law is applied where applicable, but the trauma does not end there because it is stored in memory to stay.

According to my literature review, most of what has been published in the public domain about trauma ,are topical, academic papers and books, understandable by the scholars within the specialized health care field. Most people do not have access to easily digestible fingertip facts to grasp the life transforming concept.This book is documented in a stimulating easy to understand language and example for readers of all ages. I was surprised to note that trauma is not taught in most developing countries health workers basic training curriculums including nurses who are the backbone of healthcare.

The main purpose of this book is to create awareness of existing traumas as an important public health problem in the society. Prevention is better than cure. Just as we wash hands to keep our body clean and free from invading microorganism, we need the same emphasis on protecting our mind, particularly the children in early childhood.

Trauma sensitivity basic lessons need to be taught to parents in maternal child health units to parents so that they learn to handle the newborn with care. The baby handlers at home need to know that what traumatizes a new born may not traumatize a 5-year-old child.

Policy makers need to be trauma sensitive to avoid making traumatic policies and decisions. For example, when governments take huge loans for investment which ends in loss of tax payers money, the end results is job losses and financial trauma.

A lot has gone wrong in a world that has fallen from Grace. What has happened cannot be changed. The prudent thing to do is to be informed, acquire insight through knowledge and be empowered to move forward.

Human beings have evolved from many problems that has threatened mankind through self-awareness. I am strongly convinced that if the parents who brought up those who start wars that results in the destruction of human beings creating the pain, we see was trauma sensitive, the situation would be handled differently.

The knowledge of this book will open our eyes to locate the part of the brain where anger is situated and help us to be able to avoid raising angry children in our environment unknowingly. Reading and understanding this book is a one step toward a better world for today and tomorrow.

The book has a narration of the authors traumatic childhood experience from a village in central Kenya and a mother whose child was shot to death in the state of Virginia, USA. Loss of a loved one from a gunfire is an experience no one wishes even for the greatest enemy.

Traumas are created by human beings.The same human beings can end trauma through, education, self awareness, behavior change and empowerment. A good example is how the world was able to control and suppress covid infection.

1

LIFE EXAMPLE OF TRAUMA GENESIS IN A NUCLEAR FAMILY AND ITS LONG-TERM IMPACT.

I opened my eyes at birth to a world of progressive domestic violence, rejection and scarcity of food as evidenced by a chronic diagnosis of kwashiorkor, a word I was used to hearing before I could read and write. The unending violence ended up in my late mother and her last two babies, my brother and I, being thrown out of home when I was 7 years old. We were internally displaced in our own village. We begged for shelter and food from home to home.

"An Angel of the Lord visited me at night and told me to educate the two boys although they are not mine" stated my late 42 years old father in January 1980, in a gathering of village catholic church members invited at his house. This was after my brother and I had passed our certificate of primary education exam which was a big deal by then, with flying colors making us the talk of the village. That statement knocked me like a bomb and altered my future. I was so Traumatized. My father kept his word and educated us through high school. After high school, I left home and started my life but the painful bitter traumatic childhood experience followed me wherever I went for many years until I learnt about trauma.

The first thing that I noted was that my perception of life was different from others (Realization). Among my behavior, was mistrust and restlessness. I always felt like it could happen again, like I could find myself homeless again. I was also able to distinctly identify specific clear symptoms that were consistent with reaction from my deeply rooted traumatic past experiences like extreme anger, alcoholism and walking with face down in shame. These characteristics affected my family as I redirected all the family income to address the problem of the past which they all felt had been resolved. What opened my eyes is when I identified the transference of similar anger in my first-born son and second born daughter. They could not agree on anything. They had persistent verbal and physical aggression against each other. Self-awareness of my childhood traumatic past helped me to heal the relationship between my father and I, ending up in being awarded full rights of a son in his family. My children's traumatic symptoms also resolved and they became each other best friends. Overcoming the above listed traumatic experiences has taught me important lessons that I share in this book.

CHAPTER 2

GENESIS OF REGIONAL TRAUMA (REAL LIFE EXPERIENCE)

Kenya has 41 different ethnic tribes who speak different languages. After graduating from college, I relocated to a different ethnic group about 400 miles away from home for settlement within one of the most beautiful and peaceful country in East Africa,Kenya where I settled and started a family.All went well until the introduction of a multi party democracy with a new constitution to hold National elections every 5 years. Another regional and more complicated threat started rising up again. Politicians used traumatic words against their opponents and non indigenous tribes, while soliciting for votes, every election year. These resulted in 5 yearly destruction of businesses, burning of houses and deaths between 1992 to 2017. Elections became a trigger of past painful losses as the victims remembered their losses in previous elections. What I witnessed retraumatized me. After 26 years, I relocated my family to the United States of America for greener pastures in 2014.

CHAPTER 3

TRAUMA AFTER THE LOSS OF A CHILD (REAL LIFE EXPERIENCE FROM A MOTHER)

There is extensive literature about trauma, loss and grief written over centuries, but none describes the intensity of trauma experienced by a mother who loses a child in a mysterious daylight brutal murder! Loss is defined as a permanent absence of life, indefinite separation of a person in the physical, demise of a body, that leaves a vacuum, a dead space, cracks and fragments in a human body, spirit and soul (Hines, 2016). Death due to gun violence is a called a homicide, a murder, non-justifiable, inexcusable act, where a person inflicts gun injuries to another, causing instant premature death. This causes sudden intense trauma, instant separation, and a cascade of traumas that affect the family, community and a country. All humanity is vulnerable to trauma that is not mitigated, recognized, or managed appropriately. Humans endure such trauma due to lack of knowledge, forum to express the trauma, and the culture of "you need to get over this and get on with life." I will describe the short-term effects of trauma due to loss of a son, the mother's perspective of trauma due to loss and share personal examples of how trauma affects a mother after loss of a child.

This is a true story of Dr. Jennifer Kilel, who is a contributor and peer reviewer of this book. I lost my son from gun violence in March 2023. The chapter demonstrates the intensity of trauma experienced after loss of the only son at aged 20 years. The boy had just completed his twelfth grade and preparing to go to college in the year he died. Justice was a brilliant child on the list of National Society of High School scholars, an artist (a composer and singer), a farmer and an environmental activist. He was very active in the family, community and enjoyed serving on medical missions. He had far-reaching goals and dreams that he wanted to accomplish in life all that was thwarted by his sudden death. His life was cut short, when he was shot and killed by a 17-year-old gangster in Charlottesville Virginia in 2023.

CHAPTER 4

WHAT IS TRAUMA DUE TO LOSS OF A CHILD?

Trauma after the loss of a son is acute, intense with billows of pain and swirling like a tsunami in the physical, emotional and spiritual being of the soul. The loss and associated trauma devastation is not only an immediate occurrence, but a lifelong impact of continuous trauma, loss, barrenness, shame, guilt, hopelessness and a void that cannot be filled with mere words, but trauma targeted care. Stress, loss, grief, pain, suffering, isolation, test, torture, heart break, rejection can be all lamped into one word called "Trauma", but all have different definitions as will be explained elsewhere in this manuscript. No one can accurately describe the intensity of trauma a mom experiences after the loss of a child. No one person, family or community can claim to be equipped on how to deal with this type of trauma.

What happened?

Before I can suggest how the community, healthcare providers and healthcare systems can approach the care of populations dealing with trauma, I will narrate the story of my trauma and loss briefly for the reader to understand. **It was 2 pm when I received the dreaded call from the police department that stated, "Ma'am, your son was**

shot several times in the chest, ...a period of silence...... Am sorry he did not make it!" This was barely an hour after my son Justice Kilel had left the house to go buy T-shirts in a nearby supermarket. On the fateful day, he completed his morning chores, cleaned his room, did laundry and made his lunch. Justice worked as a Certified nurse assistant (CNA) in a rehabilitation Healthcare facility for the elderly in Charlottesville VA. The police department call came as a sharp arrow thrown into the core of my existence, that left me motionless and mute for minutes. There was an outburst of neurotransmitters with a sudden overdrive actions and reactions of catecholamines; adrenaline, epinephrine, norepinephrine, and all the mechanisms of fight and flight for survival. With all the peripheral blood vessels constricted, only allowing perfusion to central organs of survival, my skin became cold and clammy as in shock, my heart rate was pounding faster and louder, my breathing was fast and shallow, my legs were weak to move, a sharp cramping pain gripped my stomach, I lay prostrate and motionless for a moment in my own urine, my inner self screaming, torn apart, with a voiceless agony that cannot be described; Justice! Justice! Justice, my son! There was dead silence and more questions than answers. Why? Why? Why? This was not a one time occurrence. It has been six months, but the trauma, the pain and the grief is not fading! Every day the loss experience is raw, affecting all dimensions of self, family, work, and community.

Trauma due to loss of a child lacks accurate terms or description. It is not a short-term problem that one can easily get over with. Loss is a subjective experience that can only be defined by the magnitude of love. I will call it "trauma due to intimacy." One is traumatized due to the love after permanent separation of the person who was loved most. To understand trauma due to a loss, one must first make an attempt to understand life, love, belonging, empathy, kindness, family and community. I can state in the strongest terms possible that the loss of a child is not a symptom that can be medicated away by medicines, neither is it an emotion requiring emotional intelligence to overcome. Trauma due to loss of a son is the direct equivalence of the love of a mother attached with a cord that carried, nurtured and protected the baby for 9 months. It cannot be measured in length, or width but only the depth thereof. There is no cultural or spiritual bypass to trauma and the pain of loss. Trauma informed care will help you understand how to identify trauma in the population we serve and create a care that brings healing to the trauma victims.

The current judiciary system, healthcare systems and human cultures have very superficial ways of describing this type of trauma and very little is in place to mitigate, manage or effectively care for the trauma victims. There appears to be a "one size fits all" phenomena approach, if there's death due to gun violence, wait for police investigation (that takes years to complete), if you have a headache, here is Tylenol, if you have sleepless nights, take Ambien and if you are depressed take Prozac. Our basic systems and cultures lack basic strategic, comprehensive trauma targeted prevention and care that can address this magnitude of trauma. If there was a system that can precisely focus on trauma, over time, this would alleviate somatic symptoms and suffering.

By ,Dr-Jennifer Kilel-Doctor of Nursing Practice

Certified Family Nurse Practitioner.

CHAPTER 5

FOUND NOT GUILTY FOR REASON OF INSANE

Statistics from CDC in 2021 Indicates that 48,830 people died from gun related injuries in USA. Out of the figure,26,328(54%) were suicides, murders-20,958 (43%) while the rest were accidental, law enforcement related and other undetermined circumstances. Anecdotal data shows that the figures increased in 2022 and may go higher by the end of 2023.

Suicides accounted for more than half of U.S. gun deaths in 2021

% of U.S. gun deaths, by type

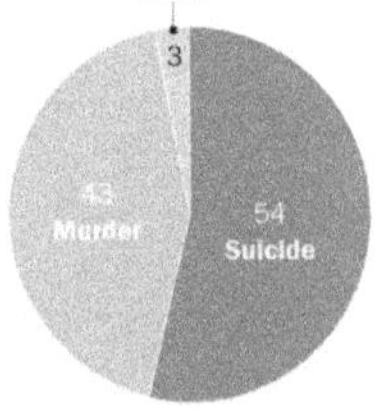

Note: "Other" includes gun deaths that were accidental, involved law enforcement or had undetermined circumstances.
Source: Centers for Disease Control and Prevention.

PEW RESEARCH CENTER

The pain experienced by the mother after the loss of her 20 years old son in the previous page is a single example of the pain that trauma inflicts on many people and alter their future.It is heart breaking to see the agony in the victims as they mourn their loved Ones. The mourners get a little consolation when the gunman is arrested and justice done. However, when the gunman kill others and himself the grief becomes more complicated. Prevention is the most important thing that we can do to stop this trend because a life lost cannot be recovered. It is hard to solve a problem permanently when the root cause is unknown. What is not in the mind, eyes cannot see.Past trauma records are not in most peoples awareness.

Knowledge can help us to live with them and control their motivated dangerous action. An individual problem, becomes a family problem, regional problem and escalate to an international problem.Trauma prevention in early life can stop this dangerous epidemic of outburst of anger. A traumatized man with limited resources is not as dangerous as a traumatized person controlling the resources of a nation.No parent know who will be the president in the years to come.We need to treat trauma prevention not as secondary to our physical body hygiene, but primary in international education sectors.

As you will learn in the subsequent chapter, traumatic incidences are gradually stored as implicit memory (Unconscious and automatic) to perform an act without thinking about it. The implicit memory can remain dormant until its triggered. Whomever we give our ears, we give our destiny. There is need for everyone to understand and identify hidden trauma so that we understand when trauma is speaking and giving a command to take an action, like fight, shoot or commit suicide. Nobody is safe until the hidden traumatic events are named. Many family members have woken up to a surprise when the least expected loved one commit murder or suicide. I obtained my second job in a psychiatric hospital after relocating to USA and was deployed in a longterm care unit. Most of the patients are calm and well educated .You cannot pick anything near the action that made them be hospitalized.They lived a very normal life in the community and never thought in their wildest dream that they would end up spending decades confined by the law. One day changed their future. Past trauma overtook them and they injured someone or committed murder.They underwent many years of court battles. Eventually, the judge found them not guilty for reasons of insane. Some of them abused drugs like marijuana to help them live with unbearable painful traumas and ended up with mental illness.

The bad news is that they were classified as dangerous to themselves and others. Therefore, they were put in confinement away from the community for the safety of others and themselves. A copy of this book can sve a family member or a friend from entering it such a complicated situation.

CHAPTER 6

WHY TRAUMA?

About 6 out of 10 men (60%) and 5 out of every 10 women (50%) experience at least one trauma event in their lifetime (center for PTSD,2020) WHO,2013 ,In a study of 21 countries observed that more than 21.8% of respondents had experienced violence,17.7% had experienced accidents and 16.2 % had been exposed to war.12.5% had experienced trauma to a loved one. We are traumatized field living with traumatized client sending them to a recovery community" - Dan Griffin. Health services were not designed to recognize the impact of trauma in children, young people and adults –Harris and Fallot 2001.

For the last 30 years, concepts of trauma informed care has evolved from a variety of streams of thought and innovation. Such a system is one in which administrators and staff of all institutions understand how traumatic experience negatively impacts behavior in multiple ways. Early in life, humans are taught personal hygiene of the physical body and seldom emotional hygiene. We learnt about the important organs like the lungs, kidney and liver. However, the knowledge about the brain as the organ of the mind was very limited. Little, did we know that all the negative traumatic experiences we encounter in life will not go away but become authoritative crew members creating unending trouble for the rest of our lives. Trauma sneaks in unexpectedly and take over the control of the victim like a plane hijacker and takes the victim where he does not want to go.

Many marriages and businesses have been sabotaged by unknowingly hidden trauma. Some victims end up in jail. Trauma is not a respecter of persons. Eckhart Tolle ,2002, in his book the power of now states that emotions are body's reaction to what is in the mind at any particular moment and any other reaction is hypocrisy. We believe that we have no control of the past but in charge of our future. We work hard and do all that can be done and sometimes we don't get fulfillment. Perhaps, we need to humble ourselves and accept the fact that Ignoring the ghosts of the past does not mean that they don't exist. Experts from Healthline, believe that trauma impacts our brain and body causing our nervous system to stay on "high alert " always ready to face the next threat.

Trauma is stored in the memory and emotional centers of the brain, such as the hippocampus and amygdala. This activates the body whenever a situation reminds the person of the traumatic events. Trauma is perhaps the most avoided, ignored, belittled, denied, misunderstood and untreated cause of human suffering.

CHAPTER 7

UNDERSTANDING TRAUMA

Trauma can result from a wide range of experiences such as loss, rejection, abuse, violence, neglect, war or emotional harm. Psychological trauma is the unique individual experience of an event, a series of events, or a set of enduring conditions, in which the individual's ability to integrate his or her emotional experience is overwhelmed (SAMHSA). Experiencing a traumatic event can harm a person's sense of self and ability to regulate emotions and navigate relationships.

Sigmoid Freud stated that, the past isn't always the past. Although, our traumas are technically in the past, traumatizing experiences in childhood can't be laid to rest until the ways they live on, is deeply understood. Trauma is a wound of a reaction to a past event, disconnection and death to the present. Painful sensations to the past events, which are as painful as the real event are felt whenever the person is triggered.

CHAPTER 8

TYPES OF TRAUMA

Acute trauma results from a single incident.Chronic trauma is repeated and prolonged such as domestic violence or abuse. Complex trauma is exposure to varied and multiple traumatic events often of invasive interpersonal nature.

Vicarious trauma

A process of change resulting from empathetic engagement with trauma survivors (Anyone who engages emphatically with survivors of a traumatic incidents, torture, and material relating to their trauma, is potentially affected, including doctors and other health professionals –British Medical association

Collective Trauma

A situation that illicit psychological trauma –"violates the familiar ideas and expectations about the world of an individual or society, plunging them into a state of extreme confusion and uncertainty".

Examples are

War.

Mass violence.

Genocide.

Pandemic

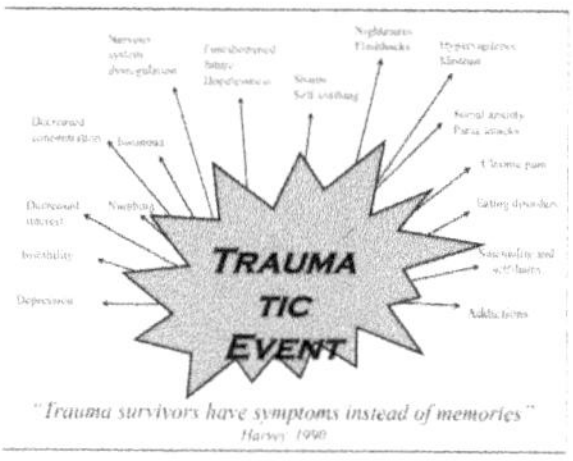

Trauma creates restlessness inside the mind of a victim and makes the individual live in a state of emergency. A person in a state of emergency cannot plan for the future. Trauma secretly and silently suppresses and ultimately terminates destiny.

CHAPTER 9

BODY'S RESPONSE TO TRAUMA

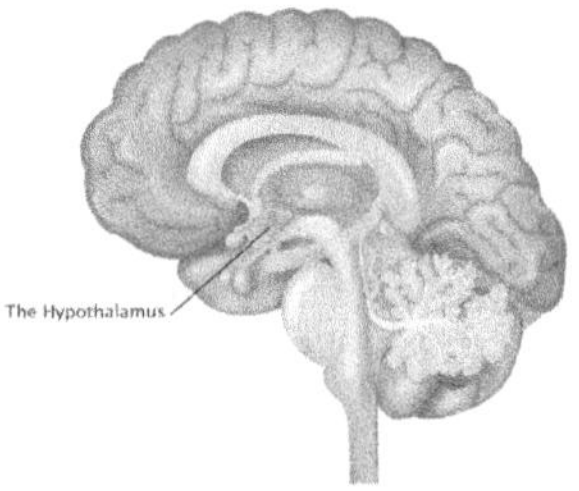

(The science of psychotherapy)

Learning about the psychology of stress, toxic stress, and trauma is liberating for people. It gives us explanatory reasons for some of the puzzling behaviors we engage in and feelings that can come to dominate us. Life throws chaos at us on a regular basis –whether it's our finances ,our relationships, or *our* health. In response, we just keep on pushing through surviving on adrenaline. According to Stanford Professor Robert Sapolsky, stress was never meant to be a 24 hours experience. You're really only supposed to feel stressed in the five minutes right before you die. When you are being chased in the Savanna by a wild animal, your stress response is supposed to save your life–it mobilizes your attention, muscles and immune system to get you quickly out of danger.

The scholar further states that, stress response is supposed to be short lived because it wears down your body, your health and your energy. It also impacts things like your emotional intelligence and your decision making. When under extreme stress you are likely to respond to situations emotionally instead of intelligently. Safety is the priority of the body. The hypothalamus scans the environment continuously, detects danger and relays warning signals to the body for immediate action before harm. This reaction is not intellectual but chemical (hormones). The immediate body reaction to danger is through the autonomic nervous system and bypass rational thinking. Human beings are primarily biologically controlled. This is the common reaction for survival that safeguard human beings and animal in the unsafe world we share. Fearful, sad and threatening stimuli including detection of threats and activation of appropriate fear related behaviors in response to threatening stimuli, occurs at part of the brain known as amygdala. This part of the brain further, helps to store memories of events and emotions so that an individual may be able to recognize similar events in the future.

The amygdala functions like a smoke detector or a gate keeper in the body (Dr Janina Fisher, 2020). If the signals are interpreted as positive and safe, the gate is opened and entry accessed. If the signals are interpreted as negative, entry is denied and a flight or fight reaction is activated for safety. Adrenaline is released in order to increase energy. Our body speed our heart rate, and breathing to increase the oxygen and blood going to our muscles ready to face the danger. Tighten our muscles ready for use if needed. Deactivates bodily functions that aren't immediately important like digestive system. Oxygen and blood is increased in the brain increasing alertness. An emotional defensive response known as flight or fight is generated. All the systems of the body combine efforts to fly away from danger for safety or gangs up and mobilize all resources to fight the stressor.

Stress can affect the brain function. Brain has higher levels of executive functions largely located at the prefrontal cortex that helps in logical, rational thoughts, executive functions, plan, clear focus and self-regulation. This part of the brain is slow and 5 times weaker. When under stress, that part of the brain can go off.

When the thinking brain switch off, the emotional brain takes over. The body moves ahead of the thinking brain to confront a threat. When the body is out of danger, the stress level goes down and the thinking brain switch back marking the end of the emergency response. Unfortunately, by the time the victim comes to normal senses, a serious irreversible damage could have been done to a loved one or a crime committed during the fight.

Most people in jail commit crimes during these unexpected moments as evidence by the regrets and pain, they express from their actions. In acute stressful situations, the person may freeze or dissociates by checking out from the body. The victim may feel cold and numb with physical stiffness or heaviness of the limb.

For somebody in deep stress ,whose thinking brain is dysregulated, it becomes difficult to physiologically access the part of the more rational section of the brain. The person does not get a chance to rest and recover.

Depending on the severity and length, the normal physiological stress response that helps us to get the adrenaline hormones remain persistently elevated. Inflammatory cascade is created causing further wear, and terror in the body. It shows up in irritability, impulsive, hyper vigilant, hyperactive, emotional dysregulation, learning difficulties, sleep changes, immune changes and gut issues. This is what is regarded as toxic stress. Trauma is the impact felt from high levels of toxic stress.

Normal stress

We all experience stress. Not all stress is the same. We have day to day stress, like when we have a test or a busy schedule. Cortisol hormones are produced increasing heart rate, breathing and blood sugar. Our body is preparing to meet a major challenge. At the end of the task, the stress level goes off and our body is prepared to rest and have a chance to recover. During the above process, the thinking part of the brain is still in control and we can still access our rational and focus part of the brain. That is normal stress. It is positive stress and as we rise to more challenges it can help us to rise to higher creativity and help us to grow.

CHAPTER 10

UNDERSTANDING TRAUMA IMPACTS ON CHILDREN.

The primary need of any human being is Unconditional love. That means ,being accepted the way one is without any judgment. The new born depends on the gaze (eye contact). If the new born perceives unconditional love, positive, calm signals are relayed to the brain communicating safety. Happy hormones like dopamine and serotonin which promotes wellbeing are released. On the contrary, if the newborn detects rejection from the carer's eye contact or any form of abuse, distress signals are relayed to the brain through the amygdala. Emergency autonomic nervous system response is activated releasing adrenaline to generate a flight and fight reaction just like in adults. A child does not have the ability to express or execute physically the flight and flight reaction which relieves the victim. All the traumatic experiences are recorded in the emotional part of the brain vaguely because the hippocampus (brain narrative center) in the child is immature. The damaging anger continues to accumulate. By the time the newborn brain matures, the emotional brain has already programmed the body by repeated response of anger towards the trauma stored in the brain emotional center. Repeated neural activity in the body makes the body develop neuro patterns (neuroplasticity).

Neuroplasticity is rewiring of brain in response to various stimuli in the environment. The inward anger can remain dormant for a long time. Whenever, the victim meets a situation similar to the recorded traumatic events, the subconscious mind is triggered and generates flight and fight reaction as though it is happening now.

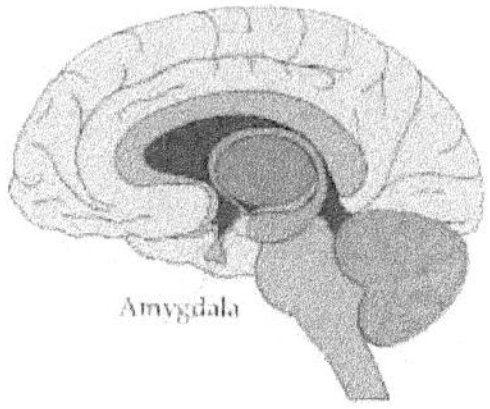

REFRENCE -Harvard Medical school

CHAPTER 11

EXAMPLES OF TRAUMA TRIGGERS

Isolation
Witnessing a related event
Being told what to do.
Lack of privacy.
Removal of clothing.
Feeling vulnerable or rejected.
Being touched or watched.
Loud noises.
Darkness
Being locked in a room.
Separation or loss.
Intrusiveness.
Transition of disruption in routine.
Condescending look

Flight reaction

The most Common flight reactions noted in the community is suicide.This is a reaction from a triggered deep trauma that is framed from inside and compels the victim to escape for survival for a better place after death.

Fight reaction

Common examples of fight reactions observed today are domestic Violence, mass shooting and wars.This is a reaction to a triggered hidden anger that creates uncontrolled energy to fight for survival.

Substance abuse

Body trauma reaction to triggers is equivalent to the real trauma.The pain is sometimes unbearable.Most victims take drugs to calm them down. Repeated substance use cause addiction with multiple problems.Some end up with mental health complications.

Trauma on mature brain

When trauma happen to a mature brain, they present as, recurrent unwanted distressing memories, dreams or nightmares (flashback).They can also present as severe emotional distress or physical reactions to something that reminds of the traumatic event.

CHAPTER 12

TRAUMA INFORMED CARE

Trauma informed care (TIC) is an approach that aims at a minimum attempt to do no further harm to the individual who has experienced trauma in their past. Specifically, it incorporates four key points (SAMHSA)

Realization

Recognition

Response

Resistance to retraumatizing.

Realization

Realization is an integral part of post traumatic experience. Its acknowledging that, one feels different from others through curiosity on how one got to where he is.

Recognition

Describes the awakening of strong hurtful experiences, which sometimes evokes feelings of guilt, shame, hurt and anger. This is recognition of the signs and symptoms of trauma. Its most important because risky behaviors like substance use and mental health conditions have been linked with traumatic experiences.

Most of the people who have been involved in gun violence have been noted to have had traumatic past that progressed to a mental illness with nobody noticing.

Creating trauma informed supportive responsive frameworks in work place can help detection of potential psychiatric patients.

Response

This is an administrative system that can respond to traumatization.

Retraumatization

This is careful attention to not create stressful toxic environments that can retraumatize individuals.

CHAPTER 13

FIVE PRINCIPLES OF TRAUMA INFORMED CARE (SAHMSA)

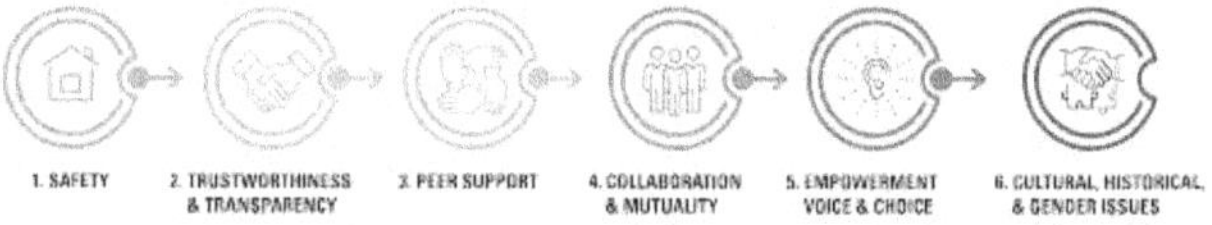

Trauma informed care recognizes that, traumatic experiences terrify , overwhelm, and violate the individual. Trauma informed care aim at commitment not to repeat these experiences and in whatever way possible to restore a sense of safety power and self-worth. The five(SAHMSA) guiding principles of implementing trauma informed care are, safety, choice, collaboration, trustworthiness and empowerment .

Safety

Ensuring that the physical and emotional safety of an individual is addressed is the first important step to providing trauma informed care .

Choice:

Informing patients regarding treatment options so they can make a choice.

Collaboration

The organization recognizes the value of staff and client's experience in overcoming challenges and improving the system as a whole.

Trustworthiness and transparency

Organizational operations and decisions are conducted with transparency, with the goal of building and maintaining trust among staff, family members ,and others in the organizations.

CHAPTER 14

EMPOWERMENT AND SELF-CARE

Learning how to regulate intense emotions, how to forge and strengthen social connections rather than being isolated, and how to develop effective communication and coping skills. Most people worldwide are experiencing traumatic financial crisis resulting from livelihood destruction from war, hostile weather, displacement, violence from gangs in ungovernable states and many other domestic problems. No government or an individual has a solution to solve this destructive phenomenon. Empower the victim by embracing the "universal precaution" and paradigm shift from asking, "What is wrong with this person?" and instead asking " What happened to this person?"

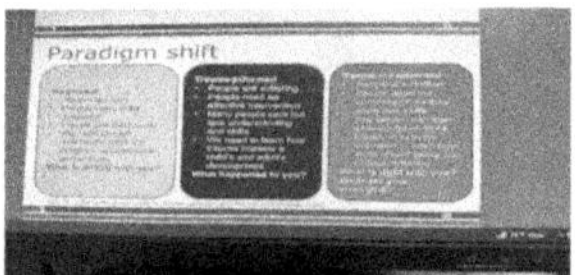

This approach is nonjudgmental and creates acceptance. Share information and create awareness to those around you. Avoid re-traumatization. Cheer up the person.

Self care

Rest
Proper nutrition
Avoid drugs and alcohol
Enjoyable activities
Setting limits
Reach out to those you trust
Journal thoughts and feelings

QUOTES

"Do not blame a person before you know how many choices he had, before he made a decision" anonymous"

"The oldest medicine in the World is love and compassion" (Vivek Murthy –MD United states General surgeon,2002)

www.ingramcontent.com/pod-product-compliance
Lightning Source LLC
LaVergne TN
LVHW010739061126
851857LV00014B/1564
* 9 7 8 9 6 5 5 7 8 5 0 5 0 *